Vera Viper and Victor Viper were best friends.
Every Sunday, Vera would visit Victor.

Vera and Victor would play volleyball...

...and watch videos.

Sometimes they would go for a drive through the valley.

Vera and Victor liked to stop in the village
for vanilla ice cream cones.

One Sunday, Vera Viper knocked on Victor's door.
"Vera, I cannot visit with you today," said Victor.
"I am very, very busy."

The next Sunday, Victor was still busy.
And the Sunday after that, too.
Vera Viper was very, very sad.
"I don't think Victor wants
to be friends anymore," Vera said.

The next Sunday, Vera stayed home.
She watched videos, but it wasn't
any fun without Victor.
Then there was a knock at Vera's door.

It was Victor! Victor handed Vera a big red valentine.
"I'm sorry I haven't been able to visit," said Victor.
"I have been busy making you this valentine."

Roses are red,

violets are blue,

I'm very glad I have

a best friend like you!

Victor read Vera the verse on the valentine.
"Thank you, Victor," said Vera.
"I am very glad you are my best friend, too!"

Then Vera and Victor played volleyball.

They watched videos.

They drove through the valley.

On the way home, Vera and Victor stopped
in the village for vanilla ice cream cones.

And that Sunday, Vera was the happiest viper
in the whole world!

How many things can you find that begin with the letter V?

See inside back cover for answers.

Vv Cheer

V is for viper and valentine, too

V is for delicious vegetable stew

V is for violin, village, and vase

V is for van and vacation days

Hooray for **V**, big and small—

the very, VERY best letter of all!

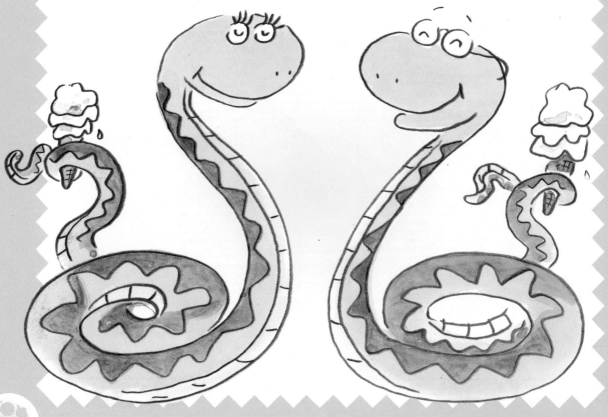